LA BELLA FAMILIA

Edwin Sánchez

BROADWAY PLAY PUBLISHING INC
New York
www.broadwayplaypublishing.com
info@broadwayplaypublishing.com

LA BELLA FAMILIA
© Copyright 2018 Edwin Sánchez

First edition: February 2018
I S B N: 978-0-88145-750-6

Book design: Marie Donovan
Page make-up: Adobe InDesign
Typeface: Palatino

CHARACTERS & SETTING

BEBE, *17, a foster child, a survivor in a Catholic school girl uniform.*

GUY, *30s, a bully. But even bullies have dreams.*

LINDA, *50s,* GUY's *mother, classless, trying desperately to be classy. She narrates her life to remind herself she's alive.*

BENNY, *early 40s, the gentlest man in the world.*

JOEY, *15,* BENNY's *son, an innocent.*

BELLA, *35,* JOEY's *mother, barely surviving in a world of violence and guilt.*

Now, and in the past.

ACT ONE

(BEBE, 17, *enters jumping rope. She crosses the stage as she sings.*)

BEBE: Guy he likes it nice
Guy he likes it tight
Guy he likes it nice and tight.

(BEBE *repeats the song until she is off stage.* GUY, *30s, pudgy, enters when she is about halfway across the stage. He strums air guitar and loud, raucous guitar music plays. She pauses for a moment, blows him a kiss and exits. He really begins to play for her.* LINDA, *50s, slovenly but with regal airs, enters, house dress misbuttoned, hair a bird's nest.*)

LINDA: Guy!

(*No response from* GUY)

LINDA: Guy!!

(*Still nothing*)

LINDA: Honey, could you possibly turn it down?! I ask him as I look him up and down. Hello? Am I even here?

(GUY *continues to play his air guitar.* LINDA *eyes him, then goes to the stereo and rips the cord out of the socket.*)

GUY: Ma!

LINDA: It's two in the morning—

GUY: This is the best part!

LINDA: I think maybe the neighbors would like to sleep. I'm practically channeling exasperation here.

GUY: Fuck 'em!

(GUY *plugs in the stereo again and continues playing air guitar.* LINDA *takes a beat, smooths her hair and rips the cord out again.*)

LINDA: Don't piss me off, Guy. I've got children services on speed dial. ...Why don't you play something soft and romantical.

(*A knocking on the door is heard.*)

GUY: (*Hisses*) Jesus.

BENNY: (*V/O*) Mrs Porter.

GUY: Knew it.

LINDA: Shut up. How do I look?

GUY: You want the truth?

LINDA: You know what they do to men like you in jail?

GUY: You look great, ma.

BENNY: (*V/O*) Mrs Porter.

(LINDA *opens the door to* BENNY, *early 40s, bookish.*)

BENNY: (*Loudly*) Mrs Porter! (*He realizes she's opened the door.*) I'm sorry. Now I'm the one making noise.

LINDA: Come in. Do. (*To herself*) Flick the hair. Flick the hair.

BENNY: No, I mean, if you folks are done with your music I'll just go back home.

GUY: I ain't started yet.

LINDA: He's done. But it's so nice to see you. You're quite the mysterious neighbor.

BENNY: Just very busy. A big day tomorrow. Joey's first day of school.

GUY: The 'tards going to school? They got school for kids like him?

(BENNY's *face tightens.*)

BENNY: He's a special boy and they have special schools for him.

LINDA: Where are my manners? *(Loud)* Bebe!! Drinks!!!

BENNY: No, I really need to get back.

LINDA: Nonsense. A little "get to know each other" cocktail is in order.

(BEBE *enters, looking down at the ground.*)

LINDA: Took you long enough. Where the fuck where you? *(To* BENNY*)* So sorry. Kids.

BEBE: I was sleeping, I have school tomorrow.

LINDA: Oh, I'm sorry. Did it look like I wanted you to answer me? Get us some cocktails.

BENNY: No. Thank you. Really.

GUY: S'matter? Don't you drink?

BENNY: Joey's alone. I should get back.

LINDA: *(To* BEBE*)* We're waiting!!

(BEBE *exits, head still down, making fists the entire way.*)

BENNY: Good night. And thanks for turning off the music.

LINDA: No problem. What are neighbors for? And, sudden impetuousness, dinner, here, Tuesday. How could you say no? I won't hear no.

GUY: She won't either.

BENNY: Uh, okay. Good night.

LINDA: Ta tas.

(BENNY *exits.*)

LINDA: *(To herself, as she touches her throat.)* Poor man. Raising a child all by himself.

GUY: Joey's like fifteen.

LINDA: All those lonely nights he must have.

GUY: The kid's a bed wetter.

(LINDA eyes GUY. Smacks the back of his head.)

GUY: I'm just saying. He's always washing sheets.

LINDA: Every night he sleeps alone, must be so hard, up.

GUY: Probably sleeps with the kid.

(Off LINDA's look:)

GUY: I'm just saying. They don't even look like father and son.

LINDA: There are still some people who treasure the concept of a family. Nobody in this house, God knows.

(BEBE enters with cocktails on a tray.)

LINDA: Took you long enough.

(LINDA takes her glass, takes a sip. BEBE about to exit, LINDA, without breaking her train of thought hits the back of BEBE's head.)

LINDA: Leave the tray and take a hike. And lock your door in case Guy should get lost looking for his room.

GUY: Ma!

BEBE: Yes ma'am.

(BEBE, barely able to contain her anger, exits as LINDA lies on the couch.)

LINDA: I hope this doesn't go to my head. I may have to sleep right here.

GUY: Why don't you go upstairs, ma.

LINDA: Ah, yes, to bed. A lonely, empty bed, lot of that going around. Our neighbor is just crying out to me. I can sense these things, you know.

(LINDA *extends her hand,* GUY *helps her up.*)

LINDA: You should go to bed, too.

GUY: In a minute.

(LINDA *stares at* GUY.)

GUY: What? I'll be right up.

LINDA: Just remember, Bebe's room is to the right and *yours* is to the left.

GUY: I know. I know.

LINDA: What you don't know is where a girl like that's been.

GUY: You're gonna lock me in my room again, aren't you?

LINDA: Mother knows best. You and I, we're all we got. Touching actually.

(LINDA *takes her drink and exits off.* GUY *looks after her. He goes to the stereo, is about to plug it in again, thinks better of it. Takes the cord and wraps it around his neck, tightening and faking his own death, until he falls to the floor. He gets up, takes the remaining drink and collapses on the sofa, lying back. suddenly* BEBE *appears with her pillow. Taking a running start she lands on his prone body and tries to suffocate him with her pillow.*)

BEBE: Why! Won't! You! Help me!!!!!!

(GUY *Flails about until he is able to push* BEBE *off him.*)

GUY: Are you nuts?!

LINDA: *(V/O)* Guy!

BEBE: When she called me I was dreaming about you.

GUY: You're on my lap.

BEBE: I dreamt that you loved me.

(GUY *stares at* BEBE.)

BEBE: Now, I don't know if you love me, but I do know that you want me. That I do know.

GUY: You shouldn't be on my lap.

BEBE: Where should I be?

LINDA: *(V/O)* Guy! *(Almost sung)* You in jail would not be a pretty picture.

(GUY *pushes* BEBE *off him and heads towards the stairs.*)

BEBE: I'm almost eighteen, Guy, she'll kick me out of the house then and get another foster kid. Do you think the next one will love you like I do?

GUY: What do you want me to do, off my own mother?

BEBE: I'm not asking you to kill her. Just, hurt her. So that I have to stay and take care of her.

LINDA: *(Shrill)* Guy!

BEBE: So that she's dependent on me.

(GUY *shakes his head.*)

BEBE: I could do it myself, but then what would I need you for?

LINDA: *(V/O)* Guy! Guy-Guy-Guy-Guy-Guy!

BEBE: I've been kicked out of every home they've ever put me in. I've been good, I've been bad, nothing works, Guy. This is it. My last foster home. Don't I deserve a place to call my own? To know that no one can kick me out no matter what? Please. You gotta help me stay. Help Bebe have a home. Just do this one little thing for me, that's all.

LINDA: *(V/O)* I'm coming down.

GUY: No, I'm coming up. *(To* BEBE*)* She's my mother, Bebe.

BEBE: Yeah, and I'm the girl you have wet dreams about.

LINDA: *(V/O)* Guy Porter!

(GUY begins to head off towards LINDA.)

BEBE: You want me? Earn me. And I'll be yours forever.

(GUY Looks at BEBE one last time before he heads towards LINDA.)

BEBE: I dreamt you loved me.

(Lights fade. Come up on BENNY as JOEY enters, his pajama bottoms wet.)

JOEY: Sorry.

BENNY: Hey, that's okay.

(BENNY kisses the top of JOEY's head.)

JOEY: I thought you went out to get mommy.

BENNY: You want a cookie?

(JOEY Shakes his head "no".)

BENNY: Well, I want a cookie. *(He begins to tickle JOEY.)* You sure you don't want a cookie?

JOEY: Okay. Benny?

BENNY: What is it, buddy?

JOEY: Carry me.

(BENNY sighs, and as best he can, carries JOEY off. Lights fade. Lights up to dim, dead center. BELLA, 35, glamorous, loads a semi automatic. she crosses herself and very professionally, she takes aim.)

BELLA: *(To herself)* Come to mama, *cabron.*

(Lights out on BELLA, up on LINDA, sitting on the couch as BEBE gives her a pedicure.)

LINDA: Hey! Careful with that thing. It's sharp.

BEBE: Yes, ma'am.

LINDA: I'm cold. Go put on a sweater.

BEBE: I'm not cold.

LINDA: *(Hissy fit)* Go put on a sweater!!!!

(BEBE *exits, returns wearing sweater.)*

LINDA: See how good I take care of you?

BEBE: Yes, ma'am.

LINDA: I'll show you how to do a real beauty treatment.
With cucumber slices on the eye and everything.

(BEBE *shows* LINDA *a tray of nail polishes.)*

BEBE: Pick a color.

LINDA: Pink. I feel like a little girl today. ...I'm bored.
Turn on the T V.

(BEBE *does.)*

LINDA: Let's channel surf.

(BEBE *switches channels for* LINDA, *while trying to paint*
LINDA's *toe nails.)*

LINDA: Even coat now. Don't be stingy. *(Off the T V)*
Nah, I don't like that program, keep going.

BEBE: If you like I can buy you some batteries for the
remote.

LINDA: What do I want with a remote? I've got you. All
these channels and there's never anything to watch.
(Looking at her toes) Just the nails, you idiot, not the toes.

BEBE: Yes ma'am.

LINDA: Stop.

(BEBE, *not sure, stops both switching channels and painting*
LINDA's *toes.)*

LINDA: *(As if to a moron)* The T V, not the pedicure.
Honestly.

(BEBE *tries to concentrate on the pedicure, but* LINDA *is unhappy with the reception.*)

LINDA: Hmm, that's not a very good picture.

(BEBE *moves the rabbit ears around with one hand.*)

LINDA: Much better.

(BEBE *lets go of the atennna.*)

LINDA: Lost it. So close.

(BEBE *again holds the antenna.*)

LINDA: There you go, that's it.

(BEBE *Swallows her rage and holds the antenna while awkwardly continuing the pedicure.*)

LINDA: I love these old movies. Oh, Ida Lupino's in this one, must be a prison picture. I'm guessing that's where you'll wind up. But not Hollywood's version of the big house, the real thing. No more slaps on the wrists for you, missy, not with your juvie record. And we both know how you just can't seem to stay out of trouble. Nice to know you'll have someplace to go when you get out of here.

(BEBE *has slowly been drawn in by the movie on the screen.*)

LINDA: Hey! Is my toe on the T V? No. Concentrate on what you're doing. That's the secret to my success. Have a goal and stick to it. Isn't that right you little idiot?

BEBE: Yes ma'am.

LINDA: Those actresses in the old movies were so glamorous. But so sad. I wouldn't trade places with any of 'em. Oh, sure they were beautiful, but they all got divorced so often. Call me old fashioned but I just think that's déclassé. One must have standards after all.

(Lights fade but stay up on BEBE *and* LINDA *as next door the lights come up to reveal* BENNY *hanging out sheets to dry.)*

GUY: Hey, why don't just put them in the dryer? You got a dryer, right?

BENNY: Joey's afraid of the dryer.

GUY: Figures.

BENNY: What?

*(*GUY *smiles.)*

GUY: Nothing. Kids learn fear from their parents. Hey, little man, you must have taught him to be a coward.

*(*GUY *exits, whistling.* BENNY *hangs up another sheet. On it is written "fifteen years ago". The sheets begin to flutter in the breeze. A glow comes from behind the sheets and the sounds of an approaching ambulance siren is heard. He reaches for a mop and begins mopping as the sheets are pulled away to reveal a hospital bed.* BELLA, *nine months pregnant, lies in the bed. He mops the floor around her, not looking at her. Very faintly a light begins to glow under the sheet where her pregnant belly is. The light intensifies, then decreases, increases again then goes out totally. The light comes back on, flickers, then stays on.)*

BELLA: *(Faintly)* …bastardo.

(The light in BELLA's *belly goes out.* BENNY *stops, looks at her, holds for a second, sees her breathing as her belly goes up and down.)*

BENNY: Lady?

BELLA: Am I dead?

BENNY: I…

BELLA: What? You're not sure, pendejo?

BENNY: I'll get a doctor.

BELLA: No. Not yet. Wait. …Put your hand on my belly. Can you feel my baby kick?

(BENNY *doesn't move, just looks at* BELLA.)

BENNY: You need to see a doctor.

BELLA: Just do it.

(BENNY *does.*)

BENNY: No, I don't feel…hold it. Yeah, that was a kick.

BELLA: Okay then.

(*Silence. An awkward pause as* BENNY *finds himself smiling at the baby's kick. He removes his hand from* BELLA*'s belly.*)

BENNY: Can I get a doctor now?

BELLA: Get a pad, *cabroncito.* Write this down.

BENNY: I don't have a pad.

BELLA: Then remember this, I, Bella Cruz, being of sound mind and unsound body—

BENNY: You're gonna be okay.

BELLA: Do hereby swear that I'm gonna kill Rey Cruz the minute I get out of this place.

(BENNY *stares at* BELLA.)

Unless I die first. You won't let me die, right…?

BENNY: Benny.

BELLA: Benny. You won't let me die, right?

(BENNY *shakes his head, "no".*)

BELLA: And you won't let my baby die, neither. Right?

(BENNY *again shakes his head.*)

BENNY: Never. I'm getting the doctor now.

BELLA: Yeah, pendejito. And then call the cops. I wanna make sure Rey is not arrested or nothing. I want him where I can get at him. And when am I gonna do that?

BENNY: The minute you get out?

BELLA: Good boy.

(Lights fade on BELLA *and* BENNY *then up on a dinner table in* LINDA's *house. She is lighting candles on the table.* GUY *enters in his usual jeans and offensive tee shirt.)*

LINDA: *(Without even looking at him)* Put on a tie.

(Without breaking his stride GUY *does a U-turn and exits to put on a tie.* BEBE *enters and begins setting the table. She sets it as if it were the grandest table in the world, and as if all the place settings were hers. even polishing a knife lovingly.* LINDA *hums to herself,* Just The Way You Look Tonight.*)*

LINDA: *(Sings)*
Just the way I look tonight, because I'm lovely—
(To BEBE*)* Remember, it's serve from the left and clear from the right. I think.

*(*GUY *enters wearing a tie over his tee shirt.* LINDA *comments without seeing him.)*

LINDA: Much better.

GUY: We should put plastic on the seats in case the kid pees on something.

LINDA: Bebe will clean it up.

(Looking at BEBE, *who won't meet his eyes:)*

GUY: …Yeah.

*(*LINDA *finally looks at* GUY.*)*

LINDA: Oh honey.

GUY: What?

LINDA: That's not how you make a Windsor knot.

*(*LINDA *takes* GUY's *tie, undoes it and begins to redo it on him.* BEBE *exits.)*

GUY: You want to sleep with him?

LINDA: Certainly not. He's a bed wetter. I wouldn't feel safe.

GUY: I meant the tard's father.

LINDA: Oh. Oh, in that case, yes. Enthusiastic nod. You jealous?

(BEBE *enters, pours water into glasses.*)

GUY: Nah. ...Should I be?

LINDA: Course not. I could never replace you permanently. You're my for always. You're dependence personified. (*She counts the glasses and suddenly realizes there are five settings on the table. Turns to* BEBE.) Can't you count?!

(BEBE *stops, pitcher in mid air.* LINDA *goes to each place setting as she identifies them.*)

LINDA: Me, Benny, Guy, and the boy.

BEBE: Joey.

LINDA: I didn't ask you anything, did I?

(BEBE *looks down.*)

LINDA: You'll eat in the kitchen. (*Feigning concern*) This is strictly a family affair, you understand? Me and my son and our neighbor and his. There just isn't anybody you could legitimately eat with. So sorry.

(*A knock on the door*)

LINDA: Get it. No wait, mine should be the first visage he sees. (*She hurries to the door.*)

BEBE: (*Whispers to* GUY) Her body moves like jello. Do you ever wonder how I would feel? How I would taste? No. Of course you don't.

LINDA: Benny and...you! How good of you to come!

(*As* LINDA *opens the door a shaft of light appears, the stage goes dark as only the tall shaft of light is illuminated. In the light,* BENNY *stands behind* BELLA, *who is in a wheelchair, her baby,* JOEY *in her arms.*)

BELLA: This is stupid. I can walk, you know.

BENNY: I know, but rules.

BELLA: Yeah, I know. The world is full of them. Benny…

BENNY: You went out last night, didn't you?

(BELLA *is silent.*)

BENNY: You said you were gonna wait until you got out. You jumped the gun.

BELLA: So to speak. *Pendejito,* stop the elevator.

BENNY: I can't do that.

BELLA: Benny…

BENNY: I can't. This is a hospital.

BELLA: Hold my baby. (*She hands the baby to* BENNY *and stands. She presses the stop button.*) Now, see, you didn't do anything.

(BELLA *sees* BENNY *looking lovingly at the baby.*)

BENNY: What's his name?

BELLA: Joey.

BENNY: Hey Joey.

(BELLA *sees* BENNY *lose himself in* JOEY. *She sits back down.*)

BENNY: So, did you? You know….

BELLA: What?

BENNY: Find Rey.

BELLA: I never knew what Rey did to make money. He said my only job was to shut up and spend it, but I couldn't do that. I always had a fresh mouth. My father couldn't beat it out of me and he warned Rey, "If you marry Bella you're gonna have to slap her around everyday cause she don't know how to be quiet. She just don't know her place." All my life men have been telling me to shut up, but I just can't do it. Even when it meant a beating, I still couldn't do it.

BENNY: Why didn't you just run away?

BELLA: *Cabroncito, t*hat's why I was in here when we met, cause I tried to leave the *hijo puta.*

VOICE: Is there a problem with the elevator?

BELLA: Yeah, it's not moving, Einstein.

BENNY: I think we're stuck.

VOICE: Okay, we'll take care of it.

BENNY: How about your mother?

BELLA: How about my mother what? She said it was a good thing I dropped the charges against Rey cause a wife belongs to her husband. I'm laying there, hooked up to a bunch of machines and Rey, my father and my mother, the holy trinity, are all yammering away at me. Rey saying he can't wait to get me home. Me and the baby. And all the while they're talking I'm just looking straight up at the ceiling. There's a little dot up there. So tiny. I'm just concentrating as hard as I can on it. Making a straight line between me and the dot. I did that everyday. For hours. Last night I snuck out and went to the social club where Rey hangs out. It was quiet, there was only three people there. And I walk in and say, "Rey, I'm here to kill you". Then I pull out a gun that he thought he had hidden so well. The other two guys get up, about to go for their pieces, but a Buddha like guy, he says "No, no. This is between a married couple. Let them sort it out." And Rey, looking so fine, he just smiles, pulls out his gun, he's so sure I'm gonna miss. "Ladies first." And I just place the dot right between his eyes. It was easy, you know. It was… easy. The look on Rey's face. How could I be better than him? I thought the other guys were gonna kill me, or at least call the police, but they're all looking at Rey on the floor, admiring my craftsmanship. And Buddha Guy, he says to me, "You want your late husband's old job?" And I said sure. "Don't you want to know what it is?" I said, "I know what it is. It's killing people, right? I can do that."

(BELLA *gets up, releases the stop button on the elevator, it begins to move.*)

BELLA: I can do that. Hey Benny, when I got back here you were sleeping in my bed to make it look like I was still here.

(BENNY *looks down.*)

BELLA: Way to watch my back. Gimme him.

(BENNY *hands* JOEY *to* BELLA, *has to help her hold the baby correctly.*)

BELLA: Take care of yourself. Okay?

BENNY: Yeah.

BELLA: Benny. You're the only one I can trust.

(*The lights return to normal as* BELLA *exits stage carrying* JOEY. BENNY *and the teenage* JOEY *take their seats at the dinner table, mid conversation.*)

LINDA: Firm believer. Absolutely firm believer in spare the rod and spoil the child. There is no gray in morality. Black or white, those are the options.

(BEBE *is clearing the plates from one course,* LINDA *makes sure to move constantly from side to side making it close to impossible for* BEBE *to clear her plate.*)

BEBE: Excuse me, are you done?

(LINDA *raps* BEBE's *hand with a spoon.*)

BENNY: (*Concerned for* BEBE.) Hey!

LINDA: (*Crisp*) So sorry. (*Feigned concern*) I've tried so hard to teach her manners.

JOEY: Water.

LINDA: *(To* BEBE*)* You heard our guest. Water.

BENNY: Actually, I try not to give him too many liquids right before bed time.

GUY: *(Passing his own filled glass to* JOEY*)* Here you go.

LINDA: Isn't that sweet? They're bonding. So how long was this house empty before we moved in?

BENNY: An older gentleman lived here. A teacher I believe. He kept to himself; we did too, so we never saw much of him.

GUY: He croaked, right?

BENNY: He had an accident.

GUY: Musta had a cat, we can't get the smell of cat piss out of here.

LINDA: That's how we got our poor little Bebe. Her parents died and the agency begged me to take her. I've always had foster children. They bring so much into one's life. Of course, those are the good ones. Every so often you're saddled with a petulant, rude little girl who you have to break, but that's what makes it so fulfilling. You get to mold the future young ladies of America. And Bebe helps Guy so much; he's on disability, you know.

GUY: I jumped off the roof on my bike. Fucked up my bike.

BENNY: Why would you do that?

GUY: *(Shrugs)* It was cool.

LINDA: Oh my, my, my, my, my, I feel like you know everything about us and we don't know anything about you.

BENNY: Well, uh, you know, just neighbors.

LINDA: And your wife? Joey's mother?

(JOEY *begins to cry.* BENNY *immediatley goes to him.*)

BENNY: Hey buddy.

GUY: Christ, the tard's a cryer.

(JOEY *leans forward, crying into his plate, getting food all over his face.*)

GUY: Gross!

BENNY: *(To* JOEY*)* Come on. *(To* LINDA*)* We should leave.

LINDA: What about my dessert? I was planning on having dessert!

BEBE: I'll clean him up.

(LINDA *beams as* GUY *objects.*)

GUY: That's what the tard's father is for.

BENNY: Could you please not call him that?

LINDA: Yes, Guy, I mean, really, what if he were your brother you wouldn't like someone calling him that now would you of course you wouldn't now apologize before I stick this fork in your eye.

GUY: Sorry.

LINDA: *(To* BENNY*)* Okay, it lacks in sincerity, but it was speedy. *(To* BEBE*)* Good initiative taking. Take little what's his name and clean him up.

BEBE: Yes ma'am.

BENNY: He really doesn't like to go with strangers.

(BEBE *puts her face very close to* JOEY's. *Whispers:*)

BEBE: Psst. Don't you want to come with me?

(GUY *slams his fork on the table.*)

BENNY: We should just go home.

LINDA: Nonsense!

(BEBE *extends her hand to* JOEY. *He takes it.*)

BEBE: It'll just be a second.

LINDA: Take your time.

(BEBE *and* JOEY *exit.* GUY *rises, looks after them.*)

Kids. They sure keep you hopping.

BENNY: Yeah.

LINDA: So tell me, Benny, what's that short for,
Benjamin? Bernard?, now that we're alone.

(GUY *coughs. Sits*)

LINDA: Tell me all about you. I'm just fascinated by
you.

GUY: Yeah, how do you make your money?

LINDA: Guy!

GUY: You stay at home, you don't go out. I think you
got yourself a website where you show yourself doing
the nasty with the kid.

(BENNY *stands suddenly, knocking his chair back.* GUY
smiles as BENNY *swallows and sits back down.*)

Hey, don't be growing balls on me.

LINDA: Keep a civil tongue in your mouth, Guy. If you
want to keep your tongue at all.

(GUY *is instantly quiet.*)

LINDA: I guess your son isn't a discipline problem,
but Guy here is, just a little bit. Sure he's a bully, but
even bullies have dreams. I think. But, we were talking
about you. Let's not beat around the bush unless of
course it's mine I'm kidding no I'm not you must get
awfully lonely. The second I saw you I said to myself,
"my dear, there is the loneliest man in the world".

(*Lights fade on them up on bathroom where* BEBE *and* JOEY
are. He sits sucking his thumb, as BEBE *very gently washes
his face with a wash cloth.*)

BEBE: You got nice eye lashes.

(JOEY *just stares at* BEBE.)

BEBE: I'm just saying is all. How old are you?

JOEY: Four.

(BEBE *smiles*.)

BEBE: Big one for your age, aren't you? I saw how you cried, you really miss your mommy, don't you?

(JOEY *looks down*, BEBE *puts his head on her chest, smooths his hair, comforts him*.)

BEBE: I miss mine, too. I think that's the one person who would do anything for you.

JOEY: Benny's good.

BEBE: Yeah, he looks like a nice guy.

(JOEY *nods*.)

BEBE: What do you do all day?

JOEY: Play. I watch T V. Benny teaches me.

BEBE: Oh yeah? What?

JOEY: Read. A little. I color in books.

BEBE: That's nice. I like that, too. I wish I could come over and color with you. Would you like that?

(BEBE *kisses* JOEY's *forehead. He laughs and pushes her away*.)

BEBE: Do you want to play house?

(*Lights dim on* BEBE *and* JOEY, *up on dining room*.)

LINDA: Guy's a virgin, you know, no of course you don't.

GUY: Ma!

LINDA: Never been with a woman.

GUY: Ma!

LINDA: Never, ever, ever. Can you imagine that? Well, of course you can't, you actually have a libido one hopes. My husband passed in a boating mishap. How did you lose your wife?

BENNY: ...I don't have a wife.

LINDA: Joey's mother?

BENNY: ...We've never been married.

(LINDA's face hardens. She becomes a stern school marm.)

LINDA: Oh? So you're living in sin? Guy, go upstairs.

(GUY doesn't move.)

LINDA: You come into my house, and judge me, pass judgment on me and meanwhile you are next door raising a bastard child.

GUY: Go, ma, go.

BENNY: I think I should leave—

LINDA: How dare you sully my home! If you weren't the best looking man I've been around in years I'd throw you right out of here! What do you bench press? Think you can lift me?

BENNY: (Stands) Thanks for dinner.

LINDA: Don't you get lonely? Sometimes I listen to myself breathing and it scares me. I think I'm the only person alive, and I'm very much alive, Benny. And you are, too.

GUY: So am I.

LINDA: I'm talking about people who matter, dear.

BENNY: Joey's mother's alive.

LINDA: Oh.

GUY: So how come we never see her?

BENNY: Business trips.

LINDA: Oh.

BENNY: I should get Joey.

LINDA: Who are you to judge me?!

(Lights fade on dining room up on bathroom.)

BEBE: Oh good, honey, you're home. I missed you so much.

JOEY: Miss you too.

(BEBE kisses JOEY who suddenly, awkwardly grabs her. she breaks free and smiles.)

BEBE: Four, huh?

JOEY: Again.

BEBE: All the roses I planted came out. Isn't that wonderful, darling? And next year I want to plant trees. Trees have deep roots you know.

JOEY: Kiss again.

(JOEY tries to kiss BEBE again, she backs away.)

BEBE: No. Let's do it right. I'm the mommy and you're the daddy. Now put your arms around me. Like this.

(BEBE puts her arms around JOEY.)

JOEY: Tickles.

(JOEY moves away a bit, BEBE pulls him back.)

BEBE: Come on.

(JOEY puts his arms around BEBE.)

BEBE: Hold me really tight.

(JOEY does.)

BEBE: Not that tight. Sort of tight-gentle.

(JOEY adjusts.)

BEBE: Now, this is how you kiss. *(She leans in.)* Press your lips against mine.

(JOEY *does.*)

BEBE: You like that?

(JOEY *nods.*)

BEBE: Now open your mouth.

(JOEY *makes a face of distaste.*)

JOEY: Yuck!

BEBE: *(Urging him on)* Yeah.

JOEY: No.

BEBE: *(Sing song)* Open your mouth and close your eyes, you're gonna get a big surprise.

(JOEY *does.* BEBE *and* JOEY *kiss again. She slips him the tongue. He tries to break free, she holds him, but he is stronger and breaks it. She smiles.*)

BEBE: You're so strong.

(JOEY *looks at* BEBE *a beat. Then he initiates the kiss.*)

BEBE: Look in the mirror. Look at us kissing.

(JOEY *does. Smiles*)

BENNY: *(V/O)* Joey.

(BEBE *and* JOEY *break their kiss.*)

JOEY: Yeah?

BEBE: He'll be right out.

(BEBE *and* JOEY *look at each other.He smiles.*)

BEBE: Your face is still wet. *(She looks at the towels.)* I can't use those. They're for company and Linda says we can never use them. *(She pauses, steps behind him.)* Don't look. *(She pulls off her panties and gently dries his face with them.)* I like playing with you. You're the only one I can trust.

(JOEY *stares at* BEBE. *She balls up the panties and puts them in his pocket.*)

BEBE: Keep them. I got more.

(Lights dim on BEBE *and* JOEY, *up on dining room as she leads him in.* BENNY *takes* JOEY's *hand.)*

BENNY: Say thank you, Joey.

JOEY: *(Looking at* BEBE*)* Thank you.

BENNY: I'm not much of a cook so I really can't invite you all over for dinner.

LINDA: Which you should have done seeing as we are the new neighbors! Perhaps a romantical meal, just for two.

BENNY: But, if you ever need any help around the house, please, just let me know. Good night.

*(*BENNY *and* JOEY *leave.)*

LINDA: …Don't say a word.

*(*GUY *holds his tongue.* LINDA *grabs an unfinished bottle of wine and heads upstairs. she stops and turns to look at* BEBE.*)*

LINDA: Clean up this mess.

BEBE: *(With a small smile)* Yes, ma'am.

LINDA: Are you laughing at me? *(She charges towards* BEBE.*)* Are you laughing at me?!

*(*GUY *gets between* BEBE *and* LINDA.*)*

BEBE: *(Same smile)* Why, no, ma'am.

GUY: Come on, ma. Nobody's laughing at you. Let's go to bed.

*(*LINDA *heads back up the stairs.* GUY *holds for a moment, looks at* BEBE *who ignores him and begins to clear the table. He heads up the stairs.)*

BEBE: (Singing as she works.
Joey likes it nice
Joey likes it tight

(GUY *freezes on the stairs.*)

BEBE: Joey likes it nice and tight.

(*Lights out on* BEBE *and* GUY, *up on* JOEY *and* BENNY *crossing past their sheets hung in the backyard to get to their house.* JOEY *moves ahead. We see him take out* BEBE'S *panties from his pocket and rub them against his cheek as he goes behind the second sheet, we see his shadow and he disappears into the house.* BENNY *follows him as the words, "ten years ago" appear on a sheet. An open door way appears, it is late at night. snow falls,* BELLA *stands, her back to the audience, wearing a revealing cocktail dress and high heels. She is lost in thought.* BENNY *enters in bathrobe.*)

BENNY: Aren't you cold?

(BELLA *doesn't respond.* BENNY *exits, returns with her fur coat, he puts it over her shoulders.*)

BELLA: If I left, you know, if I just kept walking, disappeared…

BENNY: Stop that.

BELLA: But I can't. …I can't.

(BENNY *helps* BELLA *put her coat on, she still stares out. She looks in her pocket and pulls out some cigarettes and a lighter. She lights a cigarette, inhales deeply.*)

BENNY: That's no good for you.

BELLA: They say the same thing about me, pendejito.

BENNY: Come on, close the door.

(BELLA *does. She pulls a gun out of her pocket and aims it at* BENNY.)

BELLA: (*Explodes*) Don't you dare tell me I don't love him, *cabron*!

BENNY: I didn't say that, Bella.

BELLA: Who are you?!

BENNY: What are you talking about?

BELLA: Come on, who are you mother fucker?!

BENNY: What are you doing? I'm Benny.

(BELLA *drops the gun to her side.*)

BENNY: I'm Benny. Come on, sit down, let me get you some soup.

(BELLA *shakes her head but lets herself be led by* BENNY *To the table where she sits, holding the coat close around her.*)

BELLA: You're a better mother than I am.

BENNY: You're a great mother.

BELLA: I think he's not right. I think the last beating Rey gave me broke him.

BENNY: He's not broken.

BELLA: Broken, fucked up, take your pick. Joey can't do anything. He can't even sit up. He's five years old and he's gotta shit laying down on his side. And he breaks everything he gets his hands on. No rhyme, no reason, he just wanna break it.

BENNY: He doesn't do it on purpose.

BELLA: How do you know? Sometimes I'm looking in his eyes and I swear to you he's laughing at me. Even as he sees me begin to cry and shake, that little hijo puta is laughing at me.

BENNY: He's not.

BELLA: I beat him and nothing changes. I hit him so hard. I'm balling up my fist and hitting him a lo macho, you know. I'm scaring myself. Maybe I think if I hit him a little harder he'll learn. He's crying so hard, my little baby, and I fall to the floor, crying, and you know what he does? He crawls into my lap, cause he sees me crying, and he starts making these bird sounds, trying to comfort me. *(She coos like a bird.)* A fucking genius I got.

BENNY: He loves you.

(Silence. BELLA *puts the gun on the table, spins it, almost like a game of spin the bottle.)*

BELLA: He peed in my underwear drawer.

BENNY: He was angry with you cause you had been away for a few days.

BELLA: What is he, a fucking cat?

*(*BENNY *comes behind* BELLA *and begins massaging her neck.)*

BELLA: You never get mad at him.

BENNY: Sure I do.

BELLA: No. You don't. No matter what he does, what mess he makes. Even when he hits you, you just grab his little fists and kiss them. So tender. *(She begins to cry.)* Who are you Benny? ...I could have killed him.

BENNY: You would never do that.

BELLA: How do you know? I kill people for a living, Benny.

BENNY: I don't wanna talk about that.

BELLA: You know, when you fell asleep with Joey on the sofa, both of you watching cartoons, I held the gun to his head.

*(*BENNY *stops massaging* BELLA's *neck.)*

BELLA: It's not the first time I've done that.

BENNY: Don't do it no more, okay?

BELLA: I never sleep. Ever. How is that even possible? I'm so tired. It's like my bones are on strike. How did I get here, Benny? I think about killing Joey and me. The only thing that stops me is you.

JOEY: *(V/O)* Benny!

BELLA: He'll outlive us both, you know. Then what'll happen to him?

BENNY: I'll always take care of him, always.

BELLA: I say novenas and rosaries all the time. I go to church and I spend hours praying for Joey, and Joey, won't even talk to me. He talks to you, but not to me.

JOEY: *(V/O)* C'mere, Benny! C'mere. Me go caca.

BELLA: Go.

BENNY: He loves you, you know that, right?

BELLA: I hate him, Benny. I hate my child! I'm just shoring up points with God, aren't I?

JOEY: *(V/O)* Benny!

(BELLA gestures with her head for BENNY to go to JOEY. BENNY hurries out. She puts out her cigarette, picks up the gun, holds for a moment, rises, she begins to pray softly in Spanish as she puts the gun in her pocket and opens the door and walks out into the snow. Lights shift. LINDA enters, tears down the sheet and lays it on the floor for a picnic. She begins to desperately tighten her belt, trying to make her waist look smaller.)

LINDA: *(With forced gaiety)* Yoo hoo! *(Yelling back to an unenthusiastic GUY.)* Guy!

(A reluctant GUY enters, carrying a camera. BENNY enters from his side, carrying a salad bowl. LINDA stands perfectly straight, barely able to breathe.)

LINDA: Surprise! Now you didn't think for a second we'd let you celebrate all by your lonesomes, now did you? Most certainly not. Oh my, that looks yummy, what is that? if I may ask and I just did.

BENNY: Potato salad. It's Joey's favorite.

LINDA: How very wonderful for the birthday boy.

(JOEY *and* BEBE *come running in, dashing through the adults, using them as sheilds, so as not to be tagged "it".)*

JOEY: It! You're it!

BEBE: You gotta catch me first.

LINDA: Bebe! It's his birthday! Let him win! Besides he's a boy, he's supposed to win.

(GUY *sticks his leg out, trips* JOEY *who goes crashing down.* GUY *takes his picture.* BENNY *helps* JOEY *up, eyes* GUY *suspiciously.)*

BENNY: Hey, buddy, be careful.

GUY: Yeah, be careful.

LINDA: Oh sweetness, let Linda kiss it all better, and I can, I really can, okay I'll be quiet.

BENNY: You kids want to have some cake now?

JOEY: Yeah!

BEBE: No!

(JOEY *immediately switches over to* BEBE'S *vote.)*

JOEY: No!

(BEBE *smiles.)*

LINDA: *(To* BEBE.) They're so easy to control when they're young, don't get used to it, *(To herself)* I said I was gonna stop.

BEBE: We're gonna play some more, aren't we Joey?

(JOEY *nods.)*

LINDA: Sure, go play, you're young, you'll be young forever, go ahead and play.

GUY: Ma, knock it off.

LINDA: My son objects to me telling the truth, how sad. Quiet Linda, be quiet.

JOEY: Grape juice.

BENNY: Here you go. Do you want one, Bebe?

BEBE: No thank you.

LINDA: "No thank you." The little tramp has such manners, did I just say that out loud?

BENNY: Why don't we have your birthday cake now, Joey? Okay?

(BENNY *goes into the house.* BEBE *whispers in* JOEY'*s ear, he laughs.*)

GUY: What's so funny, stupid?

LINDA: Tut tut, Guy.

BEBE: Yeah, Guy, tut tut.

(LINDA *cuts* BEBE *a look as* BENNY *returns with the cake.*)

GUY: Hey wait, there are like five candles on that cake. What is Joey, like thirty?

BENNY: He's five.

GUY: (*Rolling his eyes*) Yeah, right.

(BENNY *lights the candles,* JOEY *begins to blow them out.*)

BENNY: Not yet, buddy, first we gotta sing.

(BENNY *relights the candles. All sing Happy Birthday with* GUY *especially loud and off key.* LINDA *elbows* GUY, *who takes* JOEY'*s picture.* BENNY *glowers at him, but says nothing.*)

JOEY: Now?

BENNY: Yeah, now. Make a wish first.

(JOEY *makes a wish and blows out the candles.*)

LINDA: Lovely, just lovely.

(BENNY *cuts into the cake.* BEBE *immediately takes the first piece.*)

LINDA: Bebe!

(But BEBE *very sweetly feeds it to* JOEY *as if it were a wedding cake. Everyone falls silent.)*

JOEY: Happy birthday to me!

BEBE: You got some cream on your face. *(She wipes it off with her finger, sticks finger in her mouth .)*

LINDA: Foster children are always such a surprise.

*(*GUY *grabs* JOEY *by the shirt.)*

GUY: Listen you little retard—

*(*BENNY *jumps on* GUY's *back.)*

BENNY: You let him go!

*(*GUY *releases* JOEY *and pulls* BENNY *over his shoulder, from the back to the front, and throws him on the ground.)*

LINDA: Guy! You stop right now! Stop it!

BEBE: *(Aroused)* Yes. Please. Don't. Stop.

*(*JOEY *begins to cry.* GUY *twists* BENNY's *arm behind his back.* JOEY *hits at* GUY *wildly, who pushes him, sending him sprawling.* GUY *shoves* BENNY's *face into the cake.)*

LINDA: Not the cake! Not the cake! What has the cake ever done to you?!

(Everyone stops, breathing hard, collect themselves.)

BENNY: If you ever touch Joey again….

LINDA: Please, let's not ruin it for the children.

GUY: Why don't you call the cops?

LINDA: Shut up, Guy.

GUY: I'll tell you why, cause's there's something not right between you and the kid. Maybe you stole him.

BENNY: If you ever touch Joey again—

*(*BEBE *stares at* BENNY.*)*

GUY: You'll what? Maybe I should call the cops. How about that?

LINDA: Guy! Inside! Now!

(GUY *holds* BENNY's *stare, takes his camera and takes a picture of* BENNY's *cake covered face.*)

GUY: Like father, like son. Smile.

(GUY *then turns and exits.* BENNY *comforts* JOEY *who laughs at his face.*)

LINDA: Ah, see? No harm done, Bebe say goodnight.

BEBE: Goodnight. Oh, and I had a lovely time. *(She exits.)*

BENNY: Come on, buddy. Bed time.

LINDA: Benny, …uh, little boy, would you give us a few minutes alone?

BENNY: Goodnight Linda.

LINDA: Please.

(BENNY *gestures for* JOEY *to go into house.* LINDA *begins cleaning up, avoiding eye contact with* BENNY.)

LINDA: This will be an absolute ant farm if we don't get rid of this food, Guy is tremendously sorry, he really is. *(She takes a napkin.)* May I?

(LINDA *gestures to* BENNY's *face, he holds a beat then nods, she begins to clean his face like* BEBE *did for* JOEY.)

LINDA: Children are an endless well of unhappiness, aren't they? but I do hope you'll let Bebe and…your son continue to fraternize, they seem to care for each other, how sweet, and you mustn't worry about Guy I can handle him.

BENNY: I don't think our families should see each other anymore.

LINDA: Oh don't say that, you're my savior, I know you are.

(BENNY *grabs* LINDA'sr *wrist and stops it when it becomes too familiar.*)

LINDA: When he made his wish I made a wish too, I wonder if that's allowed. Why are we alone, Benny? How does that make sense? You probably even read. I read. We can build on that. You're a gentle man, and I'm…well, you're a gentle man. Soft spoken in a world of crotch grabbing and uber masculinity.

(LINDA *suddenly kisses* BENNY, *who pulls away. They stare at each other.*)

LINDA: Well, that was unexpected. Don't wipe your mouth until I leave. Please. Must dash. (*She collects the picnic remains in the sheet, gathers it.*) If you ever want to talk or just run away together I'm right next door. Be quiet, Linda.

(LINDA *exits. Lights dim and out on* BENNY. *Up on* BEBE *who kneels by the window, her elbows on the window sill.* GUY *enters.*)

GUY: Get away from the window.

(BEBE *leans more into the window, making her skirt rise a little more in the back.*)

BEBE: Do you think my skirt is too short? (*Silence*) I don't.

GUY: It's late. You should be in bed.

BEBE: I still have to give Joey his gift. I'm waiting for his signal.

GUY: You ain't giving him nothing.

BEBE: He'll stand by the window, move his curtains, then turn out the lights. I had to keep it real simple for him. And then, I'll take off my clothes. Just for him.

(GUY *is about to grab* BEBE *by the shouldler.*)

BEBE: Don't! Touch me.

(GUY *stops.*)

BEBE: I'm going to take everything I have off and blow kisses at him. That's my birthday gift to Joey.

GUY: I'll kill him. I swear I will.

(BEBE *finally turns to look at* GUY, *then turns away again. He takes her hair in his hands.*)

BEBE: Kiss it.

(GUY *kisses* BEBE'sr *hair. Breathes in deeply.*)

BEBE: Joey's gonna love me so much he'll do anything for me . Joey will get something, oh I don't know, like that baseball bat you keep in your room, and he'll hurt Linda for me. Oh, I know I can get him to do it. And I'll be so grateful.

(GUY *closes the curtains.*)

BEBE: I should do this from the window in my room anyway.

(LINDA *enters.*)

LINDA: *(To* BEBE*)* You're supposed to be in bed. Asleep. Alone.

BEBE: I was praying.

(LINDA *looks at* GUY.*)

GUY: …She was praying, ma. That's all.

LINDA: And you? What were you doing? And don't tell me praying cause that's not gonna fly.

BEBE: Amen.

LINDA: I'm waiting, Guy, and we all know how much I love waiting, don't we? No, I don't.

BEBE: He came down for some milk. He said his stomach was bothering him.

LINDA: Make yourself useful and go away.

BEBE: Yes ma'am. *(As she exits)* You look really nice tonight, ma'am.

(LINDA stares at BEBE as BEBE exits.)

LINDA: Your stomach hurt? It's no wonder, it's God's punishment for fighting.

GUY: My stomach's fine.

(LINDA sits.)

LINDA: Lie on mummy's lap, let me rub your tummy and make it feel all better, baby, my baby.

(GUY looks at LINDA, she pats her lap.)

LINDA: When you hurt, I'm the one you should come to.

GUY: Yeah?

(LINDA smoothes her lap.)

LINDA: Who else? I'm asking you, there is no one else.

(GUY lays down, his head in LINDA's lap.)

GUY: It hurts bad.

(LINDA pulls up GUY's tee shirt.)

LINDA: Christ, you ever think of getting any sun? *(She begins to rub his belly.)* Feel good, right? Sure it does.

GUY: Mmmmmm.

LINDA: You're purring like a cat.

(LINDA brushes aside the hair on GUY's face, kisses his forhead. she drums her fingers on his belly.)

GUY: That tickles.

LINDA: Then why aren't you laughing? *(She walks her fingers up his stomach, to his chest, up his chin and over his lips where her fingers stop.)* Don't say anything. Sssh. Let's just be quiet for a little bit. We're never quiet anymore. *(Her fingers begin their journey back to his belly.)*

If you close your eyes you look just like you did when I first saw you. You still have a baby face, a pretty face, you'd look nice in make up, yes, you would. *(She runs her fingers across his lips.)* Benny and me are gonna get married. He hinted at it when we were alone.

(GUY turns away from LINDA.)

LINDA: He says he can't live without me, we were talking you know, and he was telling me how much I mean to him, how lonely his life was, as if I could understand loneliness.

GUY: He's a nothing. Why you wanna marry him for?

LINDA: He is not a nothing! and you and, …you know, can be brothers. And then you gotta protect him, stand up for him, like a big brother should. You'll probably share a room, Benny and me will have the next one and we'll have to get rid of Bebe.

GUY: Why?

LINDA: She's not really family now, is she, no she's not. And she'll be eighteen soon. She's disposable.

GUY: She's more family than that idiot and his father.

LINDA: She is nothing.

(GUY gets up and goes to the other end of the sofa.)

LINDA: Don't pout. *(She gets up and goes to the window, opens the curtains.)* This is the best for all of us and don't I have a right to happiness? You neglect me and here's this father and son who can't live without me. *(She waves to JOEY next door.)* And isn't that sweet? Dimwitty already thinks of me as his mother. *(Calling to him)* Goodnight. *(She blows JOEY a kiss.)* I think the little dummy is gonna stand there all night. *(She turns to exit.)* Your stomach feel any better?

(GUY stands by the window, says nothing.)

LINDA: Well, I'm going to bed. *(As she is about to leave.)* Is he still there?

GUY: Yes.

LINDA: That's sweet. Isn't that sweet? Yes that's sweet.

(LINDA turns out the lights, GUY remains where he is, by the window. Lights up on JOEY by his window. The room only lit by a night light. BENNY enters.)

BENNY: Hey, what are you doing up? Too much excitement for you today?

(JOEY remains mesmerized by what he sees next door throughout scene.)

JOEY: Uh huh.

BENNY: I don't know how they found out it was your birthday.

JOEY: I told Bebe.

BENNY: Ah. Sorry about the fight and everything.

JOEY: S'okay.

BENNY: Listen, I think it's best we stay away from the people next door. I'm not saying they're bad people, it's just that, well, you can't be friends with everybody. Even if sometimes you want to. You understand? That's just how life is. Are you listening to me, buddy?

JOEY: Uh huh.

BENNY: Looking at your birthday star?

JOEY: Uh huh.

BENNY: Your wish is gonna come true, Joey. You'll see.

JOEY: Tonight.

BENNY: Well, maybe not tonight. But soon.

JOEY: Tonight.

BENNY: You get to bed. Soon, okay?

(JOEY nods. BENNY lowers the lights and exits.)

JOEY: …Wow….

(Lights slowly dim on JOEY as lights come up to the last sheet, fluttering in the night air. the word "now" appears on it. Lights come up behind it to reveal the silhouette of BELLA in her fur coat. Lights up on JOEY, still kneeling by his window. The door to his room opens and there is BELLA, in her fur coat, framed by the doorway.)

BELLA: *(Tentative)* …Baby?…

(No reaction from JOEY who keeps staring out the window.)

BELLA: Joey….

(Still nothing)

BELLA: Hey *pendejito*, I'm talking to you.

(JOEY turns to look at BELLA for a moment, then turns back to look at BEBE through his window.)

BELLA: I came back for your birthday.

JOEY: *(To himself, in regard to BEBE)* Wow…

BELLA: I'm sorry. For everything.

(JOEY ignores BELLA.)

BELLA: I came a really long way. I'm not even supposed to be here. …I'm sorry I missed so many of your birthdays.

(BENNY enters, goes right past BELLA, not seeing her.)

BENNY: *(To JOEY)* Come on, you should be asleep.

JOEY: No.

BENNY: It's late. Come on.

BELLA: Hey Benny.

(BENNY doesn't see or hear BELLA. He goes to JOEY, kisses the top of his head and sees what JOEY is looking at. He pulls down the shade.)

BENNY: Yeah. We really shouldn't see anymore of our neighbors.

BELLA: I can't go until you forgive me, Joey.

JOEY: Mami came back.

BENNY: Go to bed, Joey.

BELLA: Can I hold you, Joey?

BENNY: Love you, buddy.

JOEY: Love you too, Benny.

(BENNY *exits.*)

BELLA: I love you, too.

(JOEY *looks at her.* BELLA *holds out her arms to him, slowly approaches him for a hug. He gets into bed. She stands for a moment, defeated, then stands next to his bed.*)

BELLA: I'll wait. I got time. *(She sits at the foot of the bed.)*

JOEY: ...Mami, you dead?

BELLA: Yeah baby, *mami's* dead.

END OF ACT ONE

ACT TWO

(At rise, a sheet flutters with the words, "fifteen years ago" written on it. BELLA takes down the sheet and folds it as if it were a baby. we are in BENNY's apartment. She sits in the rocking chair, the baby in her arms. He enters with a bag of groceries. they stare at each other.)

BELLA: Boo.

(BENNY drops his bag of groceries.)

BELLA: Hey *pendejito.*

BENNY: Hey Bella.

BELLA: You remembered. Benny, that's your proper name, right?

(BENNY nods.)

BELLA: I didn't have any other place to go, you were so nice at the hospital and all, so…I got your info and came here. Is that okay?

(BENNY nods.)

BELLA: What's in the bag?

BENNY: Groceries.

BELLA: Oh. Can we stay? Please.

BENNY: Yeah.

BELLA: We won't stay long.

BENNY: Can I hold him?

(BELLA *rises and gently puts* JOEY *in* BENNY'*s arms.*
BENNY *kisses the top of* JOEY'*s head.*)

BENNY: It's okay, I haven't got a cold or anything.

(BENNY *begins to make cooing sounds to* JOEY.)

BELLA: He likes you.

BENNY: You really think so?

BELLA: Yeah. *(Silence)* There's money in my purse.
Buddha man got me a job. Take whatever you need. …
Is Joey wet?

BENNY: It's okay, I'll change him.

BELLA: I'm a killer, Benny.

BENNY: Sssh. We'll need a house. With a yard.

BELLA: That's right up there with atheist as far as God's
concerned.

BENNY: And we'll paint the ceiling of his room blue,
with puffy white clouds on it. And we'll read to him
every night. Look at him. He's perfect.

BELLA: I don't want to dream, Benny.

BENNY: Sssh. I hope he suffered. I hope Rey paid for
hurting Joey.

BELLA: Don't worry. He did.

BENNY: Good.

BELLA: Benny…

BENNY: We're a family now. We're all gonna be okay.
You'll see.

(BELLA *exits.* BENNY *hangs the sheet. The word "today" is
written on it. We are in* BENNY *and* JOEY'*s backyard. The
sheet flutter gently in the wind.* BENNY *crouches down,
takes off his glasses, is about to start crying.* JOEY *enters.*)

JOEY: Benny, tie my sneakers.

(BENNY *collects himself, puts his glasses back on, smiles for* JOEY *who sits on the ground, putting one foot then the other in* BENNY'S *lap as he ties his sneakers.)*

BENNY: Let's play hooky today. Maybe we can go to the aquarium or something. How about that?

JOEY: Bebe come?

BENNY: Uh, just us. You go play for a little bit. Don't leave the yard.

(BENNY *kisses* JOEY, *releases him, then holds him again, tightly.)*

JOEY: Benny okay?

BENNY: I'm fine. Go play.

(JOEY *hurries off.* BELLA *appears from behind the sheet. She reaches out to* BENNY, *who of course can't see her.* BENNY, *from his place on the floor, takes out a letter from his back pocket. He opens it and begins to read.* BELLA, *standing behind him reads it along with him.)*

BELLA & BENNY:
Dear Benny:
If you got this letter its cause someone got me before I got them. Every time I go out for a job I write this letter to you, just in case, and so far I've been there to intercept it, but, not this time.

(BENNY has to put the letter down, he can't continue.)

BELLA: Now, whatever you do, do not claim my body. Nobody knows about you and Joey, and let's just keep it that way. You know where everything is. You got all the financial papers, you and Joey are set for life. I don't have to tell you to take care of him, cause I know you will. You'll do what's right, for him. You love him so much. And I think you loved me. I knew I was never gonna grow old with you, but I always thought

I'd have more time. I'm not sure exactly what it is we had, but, I love you Benny, in my own way. *Te amo.*
Always,
Tu Bella.

(BENNY *puts the letter away. He rises, knocks over the laundry basket. When he picks up a sheet, he and* BELLA *are holding it together. He streches the sheet out in his arms in order to fold it, as she stands directly in front of him, also with her arms out. For a moment they almost kiss, then she backs away as he folds the sheet. Lights dim on him, up at* LINDA's. *She bursts into the room, wearing white gloves and running her hands over surfaces, and finding to her great dismay, dust.)*

LINDA: Bebe!!! *(To herself)* Shameless! Absolutely *(Loudly)* Bebe!!!! *(To herself again)* Shameless.

(LINDA *notices* GUY, *still standing by the window, only now he holds a baseball bat.)*

LINDA: What's with you? I'm curious, just not very. Is baby... *(Struggling for* JOEY's *name.)* ...uh, you know, the slow one.

GUY: Joey.

LINDA: Yeah, that's the one. *(Loudly!)* Bebe!!! *(Back to* GUY*)* Is he still there?

GUY: No.

(BEBE *enters.)*

BEBE: Yes, ma'am.

LINDA: Why do we live in a pigsty?

BEBE: It's not so *(bad).*

LINDA: *(Cutting her off)* Rhetorical! Which means answer at your own risk. I want this place spotless. And who better to do it than you, since you have to be good for something besides aggravation. I use to look

like you fresh from bed. Glowing skin, sexy hair. Could
I possibly hate you any more than at this moment?

BEBE: Rhetorical?

LINDA: Okay, everybody in this room who's getting
married, raise your hand. *(She does.)* Oops! I guess it's
just me. Who knew? Well I did.

BEBE: You're getting married?

(She glares at GUY.*)*

LINDA: Guy, I can't believe you told her. She's not
even invited to the wedding. I mean, there's the groom
side and the bride's side, and once again, she's hard to
place. So sorry. So, we've, meaning you, got to clean
this place up, top to bottom, and Bebe, your expertise
with a dust pan is really going to be invaluable to us
here. And I want to start today. Now. My destiny is to
be a spring bride. I'll sweat less. Guy, come here, look
at these paint chips. *(To* BEBE.*)* Take out the trash.

*(*BEBE *exits, clenching and unclenching her jaw.)*

LINDA: Don't! Clench!

*(*GUY *looks after* BEBE, *raises the bat over* LINDA's *head,
lowers it, raises it again, just as she turns to face him,
holding up a paint chip.)*

LINDA: Exactly. *(Referring to the color of the bat)* I'm
thinking ash or sand for your and, ...help me out here.

GUY: Joey.

LINDA: *(Hitting her head, trying to commit it to memory.)*
Joey, Joey, Joey's room. And what's now Bebe's room
will become the nursery.

GUY: Wait a second.

LINDA: I'm assuming Benny's seed is clean, that the
little idiot came from the mama, so now I feel safe in
procreating.

GUY: You're too old to have a kid.

LINDA: Nonsense. And a baby will make me look younger.

GUY: You'll look like the baby's grandmother.

LINDA: …Sometimes, I could just kill you. You are so hateful.

GUY: Sure you get a new kid, shove me off to smell little piss boy every night while you breast feed the new baby on the block.

(LINDA slaps the back of GUY's head.)

LINDA: You. You are irreplaceable to me. Could any baby be as cute as you were, well, sure they could, but what are the odds?

(BEBE enters, dragging a large trash bag. She looks at GUY.)

BEBE: Do it.

LINDA: And the color for the nursery. You'll swoon! *(She looks through her chips, doesn't find it.)* It's not here! It was right here! Oh my goodness, could I have thrown it out?!

(LINDA sees BEBE holding the trash bag. LINDA rips the bag out of BEBE's hands and empties the contents on the floor, desperately searching for the missing paint chip. At first, BEBE is shocked, then she goes to GUY. As LINDA continues her frantic search, behind her and unseen by her, BEBE tries to get GUY to hit LINDA with the baseball bat. They begin a struggle for the baseball bat as LINDA finally finds the chip. she sits back on her heels.)

LINDA: There you are! Thank goodness! I could have died. Mauve. Or is it *(Mispronouncing it)* "mauve"? Isn't it dreamy?

(BEBE tries to wrest the bat from GUY, who won't release it. LINDA animates the paint chip, giving it a funny voice.)

LINDA: Hi, my name is mauve. You'll look lovely against me. Yes, you will.

(BEBE *suddenly lets go of the bat,* GUY *who was pulling it away, knocks his own head with the bat, falls.* LINDA *turns to them, sees a semi concious* GUY *struggling to sit up.*)

LINDA: What have I told you two about playing indoors? Bebe, clean this mess up.

BEBE: Yes, ma'am.

LINDA: Guy, if you're going to nap, you have a perfectly good bed upstairs. Use it while you can, before, uh, your brother, makes a pool out of it.

(LINDA *exits amid the debris.* BEBE *stares at* GUY *for a moment, begins to pick up the trash and put it back in the bag. He tries to help her, she roughly stops him.*)

BEBE: Don't! Don't help me. Now or ever. Joey will help me. He's not afraid. He's not a coward.

(GUY *picks up the bat and slowly approaches* BEBE *when she turns around and spits at his feet stopping him in his tracks. She continues to pick up the trash. He takes his bat and heads up the stairs after* LINDA, *But halfway up the stairs he changes directions and heads out the front door of the house. Lights fade on* BEBE, *up on* JOEY *in his yard, staring up at* BEBE's *window.* GUY *joins him, swinging his bat. he just walks around* JOEY, *swinging his bat in the air.*)

GUY: Psst. (*He stands directly in front of* JOEY, *blocking his view of* BEBE's *window.*) Hey, you little perv.

(JOEY *smiles, doesn't know what perv is.*)

GUY: Shouldn't you be in retard school or something?

JOEY: No, 'cuarium.

GUY: (*Mocking him*) 'Cuarium. (*Menacingly*) I don't wanna see you staring up at her window no more. You get what I'm saying?

JOEY: No.

GUY: No?

(JOEY *pulls* BEBE'*s panties from his pocket.*)

JOEY: Bebe mine.

GUY: You little thief.

JOEY: Bebe gave to me. Bebe mine.

GUY: You think so?

(JOEY *nods.* GUY *looks left and right, drops the bat.*)

GUY: C'mere.

(JOEY *smiles, before he can move* GUY *has grabbed him by the tee shirt.*)

GUY: You don't look at her no more. You got me?

(JOEY *tries to push* GUY *away, but can't.*)

JOEY: No, Bebe mine.

(GUY *takes* JOEY'*s head and shoves him under his [*GUY'*s] tee shirt,choking him as he muffles* JOEY'*s cries.*)

GUY: You ever play with her again, I will hurt you. I will rip your fucking heart out, you got me you little idiot?

(GUY *throws a gasping* JOEY *to the ground and takes* BEBE'*s panties from him. They stare at each other.*)

JOEY: Bebe mine!

GUY: The fuck she is!

JOEY: Bebe mine!

(GUY *and* JOEY *go for the bat. blackout. On a sheet the words "six months ago" appear. An ambulance siren is heard. Emergency room. A frantic* BELLA *tears in, spots* BENNY.)

BELLA: Where is he?!

BENNY: He's okay.

BELLA: No, don't tell me he's okay!

BENNY: They gave him some rabies shots—

BELLA: Oh God.

BENNY: And a sedative, so he's sleeping now.

BELLA: You let them drug him?!

BENNY: Bella. Stop.

(BELLA *stops.*)

BENNY: Breathe. Take a deep breath.

(BELLA *begins to calm down as* BENNY *talks soothingly to her.*)

BENNY: I held him during the shots. He cried, but he's okay. The sedative was just so he would sleep, you know he's a little hyper. Okay? You okay now?

(BELLA *nods. Silence. Suddenly she punches* BENNY *in the stomach.*)

BELLA: Don't you ever, Ever! Leave a message for me saying, "Joey's in the hospital, everything's under control."

BENNY: *(Recovering)* Everything was. I didn't want to worry you.

BELLA: Oh yeah, I'm all calm now.

BENNY: Come on, sit down.

BELLA: I want to see him. What happened?

BENNY: He had a little run in with the neighbor's cat. Joey got pretty scratched up.

BELLA: How badly?

BENNY: His arms and his hands. Joey was afraid of that cat, too.

BELLA: My poor baby.

BENNY: The crazy old guy next door kept telling Joey that the cat was gonna kill him. That it was gonna sneak into his room at night, while Joey was sleeping, and the cat was gonna stick his tail down Joey's throat and suffocate him. He's just a kid you know, he believed him. Joey would cry and that would make the old guy laugh.

BELLA: He's not gonna laugh when I get done with him.

BENNY: This morning Joey got up before I did, he never does that, and…he led the cat into the shed. Took some tuna salad from the fridge and lured him in. When they got inside, he closed the door. The cat is eating and Joey takes a screw driver…

BELLA: …no….

BENNY: He's a kid, you know, he didn't know any better.

(BELLA *looks away.*)

BENNY: …He killed it.

(BELLA *puts her head in her hands.*)

BENNY: He had to. He thought it was gonna kill him. In his mind he was defending himself, he's a kid you know.

BELLA: I know, I know he's a kid. I know.

BENNY: He was afraid. …C'mon, it was just a cat. That's all. A stupid cat—

BELLA: I don't care what it was. He is not allowed to kill! His father was a killer, I'm a killer—

BENNY: He is not you.

BELLA: Maybe it's in the genes, I don't know, maybe you're born being able to kill, to look something right in the eye and kill it, to end the breath of living thing—

BENNY: Joey is not like you! *(Silence)* ...I'm sorry. He's not. He, ...he won't do it again. I know he won't.

BELLA: ...How many times did he stab it?

(BENNY looks away.)

BELLA: Did he stare at it while it was dying? Did it bother him? Did he cry? Was he smiling? I need to know these things.

BENNY: He's just....

BELLA: A kid. I know. Did it bother him when the cat started screaming?

(Silence)

BENNY: He's a good boy. He did what anybody would have done. He defended himself. He has nothing to feel guilty about.

BELLA: I need to talk to him.

BENNY: No. *(He takes her hand.)* I don't want you to tell him he's bad. The world is gonna do that to him his whole life. Please. Let me take care of this, okay? Okay?

(We shift to the present. LINDA is opening the door to BENNY.)

BENNY: How is Guy?

LINDA: No one knows anything. All those medical degrees just looked at me and shrugged. I can't breathe. Guy is my baby. Did you or, the boy see anything?

BENNY: The police already asked us—

LINDA: I'm asking you.

BENNY: *(Shaking his head)* I'm sorry.

LINDA: I know, ...a lot of people didn't like Guy, he was a bit of a bully, but in a nice way. Never beat up anybody who didn't deserve it. There must have been a gang of them, of felons. They beat my baby, Benny.

BENNY: I'm sorry.

LINDA: With his own baseball bat, not that Guy ever played sports, should I still be flirting, I'm not sure, he hated gym class.

(BEBE *enters*.)

LINDA: There's the little co-conspirator.

BENNY: You shouldn't say that.

LINDA: If she had taken out the trash, like I asked her to time and time again, Guy wouldn't have been out there alone. She would have been the one beaten back to her infancy and not my baby!

BEBE: He's awake.

BENNY: You brought him back here?

LINDA: The hospital wanted to just keep him there forever, like I'm made of money. Oh, sure, I could have used Guy's college fund, that ship has sailed, but then what? He's not gonna get any better.

BEBE: I think he wants to be in the living room, with you.

LINDA: Oh good Lord, he's a drooler. (*To* BENNY) I guess you and I will be entre nousing it at the wash line. Guy drools over everything now.

BEBE: He could choke on his own spit.

LINDA: Tell the world why don't you? Can't speak, drags his leg when he walks, like a rag doll left out in the rain or something, I think that's the line from a song. I'm a terrible mother.

BENNY: No you're not.

BEBE: Yes you are. (*As she exits, she whispers to* LINDA.) Fluff your hair and wet your lips.

LINDA: Why that little trollop. *(She fluffs her hair, wets her lips.)* She's right, you know, I am a terrible mother.

BENNY: I'd like to come over later and visit with Guy. And you, of course, if that's okay.

(LINDA stares at BENNY.)

LINDA: Why? Why on earth?

BENNY: Just, to help.

LINDA: Who are you Benny?

BENNY: I'll bring him ice cream. That's easy to eat.

LINDA: Guy can't control his bowel movements, I don't know why I'm saying this, I just thought you should know.

BENNY: Depends. Get him some Depends, but sprinkle them with baby powder before you put them on him. And no liquids after dinner.

LINDA: I should be writing this down.

BENNY: I'll be back.

LINDA: I've got an anchor around my neck and now you want to come back?

BENNY: He like vanilla?

(LINDA nods.)

BENNY: Look at it this way. This is almost like a gift to you. It just means he needs you. More than ever. And now, now he'll always need you. When kids grow up they leave you. He'll never leave.

LINDA: You are a mystery.

BENNY: Nah, I'm just the quiet guy next door, that's all. *(He exits.)*

LINDA: ...Nice butt.

(BEBE enters, barely able to carry a large laundry basket, filled with bed clothes.)

LINDA: Did little Guysie Whysie go poopy woopsie?

BEBE: Ew, gross. And the dryer is dead.

LINDA: Well, that's a shame. Off to the wash line with you. But if you see Benny there, run back and get me.

(BEBE *throws the basket on the floor.*)

LINDA: You seem to have dropped your basket.

BEBE: I'm not doing this! He's your son! Okay? Yours! I don't see you lift a finger to help him! You are a terrible mother! You're the worst mother on the face of the earth! I hate you! I hate you! I hate you! *(She screams in frustration.)*

LINDA: All better now? Okay. Let's hop to it, those sheets are not gonna do themselves.

(BEBE *goes for the door, has barely touched the door knob.*)

LINDA: And don't you even think of leaving me. Your place is here, next to me, taking care of that albatross.

BEBE: I wanted to stay, but not like this.

LINDA: Like how then? As the new lady of the house?

(BEBE *is silent.*)

LINDA: This is almost like your home, dear, even an ingrate like you should know that much. And I can't live forever, now can I? There, I've thrown you a bone, now have the good breeding to pick it up and hope I drop dead soon.

BEBE: I'm not going to stay as a servant.

LINDA: Yes you will. For lack of a better word, this is your home.

(BEBE *picks up the laundry basket and exits. there is a banging sound from above,* LINDA *looks up.*)

LINDA: Mummy's coming, precious.

(The banging continues as LINDA *exits. Scene shift, to next door.* JOEY *sits, still watching* BEBE's *window.)*

BELLA: Show's over, *pendejito.*

*(*JOEY *takes out* BEBE's *panties and twirls them around.)*

BELLA: Those belong to that little *puta maldita* next door, right?

*(*JOEY *continues to play with them.)*

BELLA: Hey! I'm talking to you! Your mother is talking to you! Put those down, you don't know where they've been. Or worse yet, you do.

JOEY: Bebe likes me.

BELLA: She don't like nobody but herself.

JOEY: She like me, and Benny like me. *(Silence)* You don't like me.

BELLA: ...Joey...

JOEY: You never like me.

BELLA: Baby, that's not true. I love you so much, with all my heart and soul, I— Gimme those goddamn panties!

*(*BELLA *tries to grab the panties, but can't. She tries again, but she can't hold anything.)*

JOEY: Mommy, you like air now.

BELLA: Yeah, guess I am.

*(*BELLA *gently blows on* JOEY. *He giggles.)*

JOEY: Tickles.

BELLA: I did so many bad things. Can you ever forgive mami, baby? Can you?

JOEY: What did you do?

*(*BEBE *enters.)*

BEBE: Hey, Chucky Cheese, talking to yourself? Like you're not crazy enough?

BELLA: *Puta. Puta maldita.*

JOEY: Bebe mine.

(JOEY *tries to kiss* BEBE, *she fends him off.*)

BEBE: Easy cowboy. They brought Guy back today.

(JOEY *is silent.* BEBE *sees her panties in his fist.*)

BEBE: I said they brought Guy back from the hospital today. Nobody knows what happened to him. I don't think the cops even care. Did you see what happened to Guy, Joey?

BELLA: Don't tell this fucking little Nancy Drew nothing.

BEBE: Did you?

BELLA: Say no.

JOEY: No.

BEBE: Remember? It was right after your birthday. I gave you a extra special gift.

JOEY: Bebe mine.

BEBE: You been out here ever since. Always looking up at my window. You must have seen who beat Guy.

BELLA: Say no.

(JOEY *is silent.*)

BELLA: *Pendejito,* say no!

(JOEY *is silent.*)

BEBE: You know what I hate more than secrets? People who keep them. I don't talk to them, I don't play with them, I don't have nothing to do with them.

(BEBE *begins to hang up the sheets,* JOEY *tries to help, she slaps him. Hard. He looks down and begins to cry.*)

BEBE: Did I say you could help me? No.

(*As* BEBE *hangs up a sheet,* JOEY *runs into his house, follwed by* BELLA. *On the sheet the words "three months ago" appear. Night.* BELLA *behind the wheel. lights of oncoming traffic wash over her. she rubs her exhausted eyes, pulls out her cell phone, speed dials.*)

BELLA: Hey, did I wake you? ...Sorry. How's Joey?... Good. No, nothing. Yeah, I'll pick up some milk on my way back. Benny... I, uh, killed Buddha Man. Tonight. I walked up behind him, and he knew it was me, right off the bat, without even looking at me. He says to me, "I must still rate if they sent you. You're the best in the business." Sits there with his hands folded. He's got nice hands. Really. Small and delicate. I wish I had hands like that. I ask him if he wants something to eat or anything, I don't do that for other people, but, he's Buddha Man, you know?

(BELLA *shakes her head, a horn is heard, she steers her car back to her lane.*)

BELLA: Yeah, I'm still here. He tells me he really doesn't eat all that much and I tell him I don't sleep. And then we're kinda quiet for a while until he asks me, "How's Joey?". I thought nobody knew about Joey, I told everybody he died, I didn't want anybody getting any ideas about him. Buddha Man sees me begin to panic, not a good thing, so he says "Don't worry. Nobody knows but me". I take a breath and then we just talked about Joey, you, God. Everything. And he asks me what's going to happen to Joey when I'm gone. He tells me, make sure Joey's taken care of, put your house in order, it's the only way you'll rest in peace. Then he closes his eyes and says to me, "Do it, Bella. It'll be a relief. Trust me." So I did. ...Benny? ...I can't hear you. I think I'm losing you. I said, I'm losing you.

(Scene shift. Lights up as LINDA *is helping* GUY *to the couch. She sings.)*

LINDA: Take a little one step, one step, one step. Come a little closer please.

(No reaction from GUY, *who even through his bandages is still banged up pretty bad. He just lets himself be awkwardly moved.)*

LINDA: Honey, are you in there? *(Screams out)* Bebe! *(Realizes she's screamed in* GUY's *ear.)* So sorry.

*(*BEBE *enters.)*

LINDA: Help me sit him down.

(They do.)

LINDA: Benny's coming over later—

*(*GUY *begins to flail about as best he can.)*

LINDA: Yes, yes, I'm absolutely wet with excitement myself, but baby, baby, baby, calm down.

*(*GUY *calms down a bit, continues his labored breathing.)*

LINDA: I do believe our neighbor's coming a courting so try not to look too pathetic, and he asked to see you, isn't that nice?

*(*GUY *looks to* BEBE, LINDA *catches it.)*

LINDA: What's this? What's with the look?

BEBE: Nothing.

LINDA: Usually is. Make sure you take the dimwit and make yourself scarce. *(Looks at* GUY*)* I'm so sorry, this must be confusing for you. I meant the younger dimwit.

(A knock on the door)

LINDA: Get it, Bebe.

BEBE: I thought you wanted your "visage" to be the first thing he saw.

LINDA: Well then answer the bloody door backwards!

(BEBE, *with some difficulty, opens the door. A shaft of light from the door.*)

BELLA: Look at the brochures, come on, just look at them.

BENNY: Joey has a home.

BELLA: Every time I walk out that door could be my last time.

BENNY: I'll always take care of Joey, you know that.

BELLA: And there will be a time when you die, Benny, like everybody else.

BENNY: Not for a long time.

BELLA: How do you know? Trust me, nobody programs their V C R thinking they're not gonna see it later on. I deal in death and it's sudden.

BENNY: Everything is fine the way it is.

BELLA: No, it's so fucking far from fine! When I die I need to know Joey's taken care of. And you need the same thing. You die and you'll never forgive yourself for leaving Joey. And nobody's gonna have the patience you had with him. He'll be a ward of the state in some institution, he won't know where he is, and he'll be afraid. All these places here, they're like expensive, good places. And you can visit whenever you want. He can make friends. Come on, he doesn't know anybody except you and me.

(BENNY *knocks the brochures of* BELLA's *hand.*)

BENNY: He doesn't need anybody else but me!

BELLA: I'm his mother, Benny. You're ego ends where mine begins.

BENNY: Everything he knows I taught him! You gave up on him! I didn't. I love him.

BELLA: (*She carresses* BENNY's *head.*) Oh, Benny, I know you do, but don't you want your life back?

BENNY: Joey is my life. I'm nothing if I'm not his father.

BELLA: But you're not his father, are you? (*Silence*) Are you? I want to do right by you, Benny, I really do. But I'm his mother and this is what's gonna happen. He's going into a home next month. Period. End of conversation. I gotta think about what's best for Joey. And you should too.

(*Lights return to normal.* BENNY *sits next to* LINDA *on the sofa, who sits next to* GUY. *She is showing* BENNY *a photo album.* JOEY *sits on the floor, staring at* BEBE *who refuses to look at him.*)

LINDA: And this is Guy on his first day of school. Notice the curls? Fetching. Very fetching. Well, like mother like son, yet at our core misunderstood people.

BENNY: He looks so innocent.

LINDA: Weren't we all? (*To herself*) Leg cross, show a little cleavage. (*To* BENNY) Oh, and here we are at the beach. I'm in the barely there bikini—

BENNY: He's holding your hand.

LINDA: What?

BENNY: In the picture. Guy is holding your hand.

LINDA: Couldn't swim, sank like a stone, even with all that body fat. How about that bikini, huh? Bebe, put on a fresh pot of coffee. And take… (*She points with her mouth to* JOEY.) …with you.

(BEBE *ignores* LINDA.)

LINDA: Bebe, …angel.

BENNY: Don't bother with the coffee on my account.

(LINDA *laughs as if this had been the funniest thing in the world.*)

LINDA: Benny, you're a caution! Such a wit. And so droll, as in roll, in the hay.

BEBE: Give it a rest.

LINDA: Excuse me?

BEBE: Nothing ma'am.

LINDA: I'm sure Guy would be laughing too. If he could, I mean.

(BENNY *leans into* GUY.)

BENNY: How about it, Guy? Do you think I'm funny?

LINDA: My baby always had a great sense of humor. You just had to see his wardrobe to know that.

BENNY: Joey, why don't you give Bebe the card you made for her. (*To* LINDA) He made it all by himself.

LINDA: How very pleasant.

(JOEY *extends the card to* BEBE, *who doesn't move.*)

LINDA: Bebe…

(*A not very interested* BEBE *takes the card.* LINDA, *between clenched teeth.*)

LINDA: Read it, you witch.

BEBE: Bebe mine.

BENNY: That's a heart in the center.

BEBE: Oh yeah? Who's?

JOEY: Mine.

BENNY: Joey has a little crush on Bebe.

LINDA: I never would have guessed. Well, boys will be toys.

BEBE: Well, I don't like him. Not anymore.

LINDA: Bebe!

BEBE: I don't. He keeps secrets.

LINDA: We all keep secrets. Why you'd have to kill me to get my real age out of

BEBE: Fifty three.

LINDA: me. *(She glares at* BEBE.*)*

BENNY: I don't care about that.

LINDA: Oh sure, men never do.

BENNY: No, really. I mean, I look at you and I don't see a number.

LINDA: What do you see?

*(*BEBE *lets the card fall to the floor.* GUY *begins to hit* LINDA*'s shoulder with his head.)*

LINDA: Guy!

*(*BENNY *tenderly holds* GUY *back.* GUY *freezes in fear.)*

BENNY: Hey, easy. Easy, buddy. Don't want to hurt yourself.

LINDA: He's gotten so excitable. He could barely contain himself when I told him you were coming. Oh great, he got drool on me. I'll have to freshen up. *(She rises.)* Oh, and Bebe, I'm sure you want to tell Benny you were only kidding when you said I was—

BEBE: Fifty three.

LINDA: —that age.

*(*LINDA *glares at* BEBE *as she exits.* BEBE *takes her place next to* GUY *on the couch.)*

BEBE: Your ice cream should be soft enough now.

BENNY: Can I feed him?

BEBE: He's not a dog.

*(*GUY *shakes his head "no" as best he can.)*

BENNY: I didn't mean that. He's just like a little baby now, that's all. Like my Joey.

JOEY: I'm not a baby.

BEBE: ...Joey, you wanna come with me and get some ice cream?

JOEY: Yeah.

BEBE: Come on.

(BEBE and JOEY exit. BENNY picks up the bowl of ice cream, mashes it, smiles at GUY.)

BENNY: So, how you feeling, Guy? You look pretty good.

(GUY is petrified.)

BENNY: Getting nice and soft, just like you like it. Hey Guy, how about you and me here on this couch. How about that? *(Sees the camera on the table next to them.)* Is that your camera? Aw gee, let's take a picture of us. *(Holding the camera away from them, he puts his face near GUY's, smiles.)* Smile.

(The flash goes off, brief blinding light and the sound of a bat hitting a skull is heard.)

(BENNY puts the camera down, picks up a spoonful of ice cream.)

BENNY: Oooh, here comes the airplane. Open up the hangar.

(BENNY flies the spoon around, heads for GUY's mouth which remains tightly shut. BENNY stares at him for a moment, smiles.)

BENNY: You okay, buddy? Hmm?

(BENNY puts the spoon back in the bowl, takes his fingers and gently pries open GUY's mouth. GUY begins to cry.)

BENNY: Hey. Hey, it's okay. I'm right here. I'm not going anywhere. And you know, that incident with the baseball bat, we never have to talk about it. Ever. That can be our little secret.

(The flash goes off, brief blinding light and the sound of a bat hitting a skull is heard. GUY *nods "yes" as best he can.)*

BENNY: You know, people always push the little guy, cause they think he'll never push back. But it feels good to push back. It really does. *(He picks up the spoon again.)* Here comes the airplane again. Zoom. Zoom.

*(*GUY *closes his mouth.)*

BENNY: Open your mouth, buddy. You don't want to make Benny angry. Not again.

*(*GUY *slowly does. He lets himself be fed ice cream.)*

BENNY: That's my good boy. I'll take care of you. Yes, I will.

(Scene shift. BEBE *and* JOEY *enter hallway, she immediately grabs him and kisses him then pulls away.)*

BEBE: Okay, okay, easy.

JOEY: Bebe mine.

BEBE: We'll see. Let me do the kissing. Put your hands behind your back.

*(*JOEY *tries to embrace her, she slaps his hands away.* JOEY *looks as if he's about to cry.)*

BEBE: Hey. *(Gently)* Hey.

*(*BEBE *kisses* JOEY's *hand.* BELLA *enters, watches.)*

BEBE: Tell you what. Let's play a little game. For every question you answer I'll give you a kiss. You like that?

*(*JOEY *nods.)*

BEBE: You know what happened to Guy, don't you?

BELLA: Joey, no.

*(*JOEY *doesn't answer.* BEBE *purses her lips together, kisses the air.)*

BEBE: Don't you?

JOEY: Uh huh.

BELLA: That's enough, Joey.

BEBE: He got beaten with a baseball bat.

JOEY: Uh huh. Kiss please.

BEBE: That wasn't a question. Now, I think, I think it was either you or Benny. Am I right?

(JOEY is silent.)

BELLA: No. Say "no"!

JOEY: No.

BELLA: *(To BEBE, who of course can't hear her.)* Hah! Go to hell!

BEBE: If you lie, that's cheating. And I'll never play with you again.

(Silence)

BELLA: *(Whispers into JOEY's ear.)* Say, "I'm not lying".

JOEY: Not lying.

(BEBE gives JOEY a long, romantic kiss. She gently takes his face in her hands, he tries to do the same, she stops him.)

BEBE: Hands behind your back.

(JOEY puts his hands behind his back. BEBE gives him little kisses all over his face.)

BELLA: Joey, please, just go. Get out.

BEBE: Was it Benny?

(JOEY looks down.)

BEBE: Come on. You know. Just tell me that Benny did it and you and me can be together forever. Wouldn't you like that? Cause I know there's more to Benny than he lets on. Nobody's that good.

(JOEY begins to cry. BELLA kisses the back of his head. BEBE kisses JOEY, hard.)

BEBE: That was it. That was the last kiss. Savor it. Remember it. Put it in your little fucking retard scrap book.

(BEBE *makes as if to leave,* JOEY *blocks her.*)

JOEY: *(Gently)* Bebe, please…

BEBE: It would have been one thing for Linda to wind up like a dribbling idiot, Guy would have taken care of her. But now? I either get tossed out on the street or I spend the rest of my life changing Guy's dirty diapers. Benny, or you, one of you put me in this position. Look at me! Now, if it was you, they'll lock you up in some loony bin, but maybe it was Benny. Maybe he just couldn't take Guy no more. If he did it they'll take him away and you'll be left all alone. Too bad. So sad.

BELLA: Joey, don't say anything.

BEBE: One of you screwed me out of my place at the table. Who was it?!

(JOEY *is crying softly.*)

BELLA: Sssh.

BEBE: *(Gently)* Sssh. You can tell me. I'm your Bebe.

BELLA: Tell her, "mami did it".

(JOEY *turns, looks at* BELLA.)

BEBE: Hey, I'm over here.

(JOEY *turns to* BEBE.)

JOEY: *Mami* did it.

(*Scene shift.* LINDA *reenters living room. from her perspective sees a touching tableau of* BENNY *feeding* GUY *ice cream.*)

LINDA: It's very sweet of you to be so kind to Guy. He doesn't inspire much kindness. Where are the children? My, don't I sound everyday kind of normal?

BENNY: Getting ice cream. I worry sometimes Bebe may be too old for Joey to play with.

LINDA: Bebe's too old for a killer shark. When Guy was a little boy I used to take him to the beach. He'd always get burnt because he refused to put on sun tan lotion. He said it was girly. He never became a man. Just an old boy. That's not too attractive. And now of course he's a root vegetable.

BENNY: You shouldn't say that. And you know, you can always count on me to help you.

LINDA: Why? ...I'm not stupid, Benny.

BENNY: I never said you were stupid.

LINDA: I mean I'm pathetic, horny and I'm no spring chicken, but I'm not stupid. For you to even consider helping us—

BENNY: Did I tell you, you look nice tonight?

LINDA: —is ridiculous. Oh, you think so? *(She goes to the mirror, checks herself.)* I was worried the neckline might have been a tad too much.

(BENNY reaches into his pocket and takes out a comb, he begins to comb GUY's hair. LINDA sees this.)

LINDA: Were you talking to me or the paper weight?

(BENNY covers GUY's ears.)

BENNY: He can hear everything. Isn't that right, buddy?

(GUY tries his best to jerk his head away but BENNY holds it firmly in place.)

BENNY: Wanna make you look nice and spiffy.

LINDA: Getting back to me not being stupid, how was it that neither you or...Joey, finally! heard or saw anything when Guy was beaten up?

(BENNY continues to comb GUY's hair.)

BENNY: Just didn't. That's all.

(LINDA *stares at* BENNY *with* GUY, *she softens.*)

LINDA: I see you sitting there with Guy, so gentle and kind and it reminds me of everything that's missing in my life. I know, I'm the town joke.

BENNY: No, you're not.

LINDA: Please. It's not a pleasant thing to admit, but even I can deny just so much. You're a little piece of heaven so you wouldn't know this but monsters are made not born oh boy I'm ready for a cocktail, my first husband, Guy's father, well imagine Guy squared. The only way he liked his sex was if it came gift wrapped in a bruise. I'm being indelicate or I'm being honest, take your pick. Guy is definitely his father's son.

BENNY: We can change that.

LINDA: But this I promise you, I simply will not rest until whoever did this is behind bars where they belong.

BENNY: …You know, you and I should get married.

LINDA: What? Come again. Hopefully.

BENNY: Well, I've been very lonely since my wife died.

LINDA: Whoa. Wife?

BENNY: Joey's mother.

LINDA: You weren't married to her.

BENNY: Of course I was.

LINDA: You sat right here and told me you weren't.

BENNY: I never said that.

LINDA: You most certainly did. I…I…I…

BENNY: (*Close enough to taste her.*) No. I didn't.

LINDA: (*Losing herself in him*) Oh, …I, I must have misheard you.

BENNY: You must have. Cause Joey's my son, my birth son. *(Looks at* GUY*)* And no one can prove any different.

(Scene shift, back to BELLA, BEBE *and* JOEY.*)*

BELLA: Say, "*Mami* came back for me."

JOEY: *Mami* came back for me.

BELLA: She saw Guy and she beat him up.

JOEY: She beat Guy.

BEBE: Why? Why would she?

*(*JOEY *is silent.)*

BELLA: Because *mami's* bad.

JOEY: *Mami* bad.

BELLA: She, …she don't love nobody.

*(*JOEY *doesn't repeat this.)*

Baby…It's okay. Just say it.

JOEY: *Mami* gone. Not come back.

BEBE: You hope.

BELLA: No. She's not coming back.

JOEY: Not coming back.

BEBE: Why not? She dead or something?

*(*JOEY *nods.)*

BELLA: Kiss her. You know you want to.

*(*JOEY *kisses* BEBE.*)*

BELLA: Gentle.

*(*JOEY *kisses* BEBE *again, this time gently. As they pull apart, she looks at him, smiles, is about to say something.)*

BEBE: You're—

BELLA: Kiss her again.

*(*JOEY *does.* BEBE *softly touches her lips.)*

BEBE: ...I thought I was driving this car. Come on, I'll get you that ice cream.

(JOEY *smiles.*)

BEBE: Okay, Bebe yours.

(BEBE *exits.* BELLA *Blows on* JOEY's *head, he remains.*)

BELLA: Can you forgive me, Joey? Please.

(JOEY *suddenly hugs* BELLA.)

BELLA: I'm air, baby, you can't feel me. You take care of yourself, and listen to Benny. He'll look out for you. He's the only one I can trust.

(*Scene shift. Back to* BENNY, LINDA, *who are about to kiss.*)

LINDA: Boy, you think you know a person.

(GUY, *who uses his last bit of strength to knock down the vase by his side. Flowers scatter on the floor.*)

LINDA: Guy! Look at this mess! (*Screams out*) Bebe!

BENNY: Are you okay, buddy?

LINDA: He's fine. Just spastic. Well, Benny, Ben, Ben, Ben— (*She gets on her hands and knees, cleaning up the mess, picking up the flowers.*) It pains me a great deal to say this, but you don't love me.

(BENNY *gets down on one knee.*)

BENNY: Linda—

LINDA: Good Lord, he's going for the gold.

BENNY: I know all I am is the little guy next door, but let me take care of you. I'm good at it. You'll see. Please will you marry me?

LINDA: Are you sure? Why am I even giving you a chance to back out?

BENNY: How about it, Guy? Can I have your mother's hand in marriage?

(GUY *uses all his strength to violently shake his head, "no".*)

LINDA: Guy!

BENNY: He's forgotten how to say yes. But don't worry.
I'll teach him.

LINDA: I really should entertain other offers, but I'm
so saddened by your loneliness, your need, so yes, I'll
marry you, Benny. And if that makes me a saint, so be
it.

(LINDA *reaches out to kiss* BENNY, *who kisses her and hugs*
GUY *with a free arm.*)

BENNY: This is just great.

LINDA: Guy, you have a new daddy!

BENNY: And I'll take care of you for the rest of your life.
How about that?

(BEBE *and* JOEY *enter.*)

BENNY: There's my boy! (*He hugs* JOEY.) Come on, say
hello to your new brother.

(BENNY *leads* JOEY *to* GUY.)

BENNY: Wait, let me get a picture of you two.

(BENNY *takes the camera, snaps a picture as* JOEY *punches*
GUY. *The flash goes off, bright light.* GUY *grimaces.*)

LINDA: He just hit Guy!

BENNY: Just a little horse play between brothers. Boy,
that dress. Have I told you how nice you look tonight?

LINDA: And let's have a shot of me and my betrothed.
Is that even a word?

BENNY: First a shot of me and my boys.

(BENNY *hands the camera to* LINDA *and sits with an arm*
around GUY *and* JOEY.)

LINDA: (*A little disappointed*) ...Oh yeah, let's get that
one first.

BENNY: My two sons. Mine forever. *(To* GUY*)* Ain't that right, buddy?

JOEY: I'm buddy.

BENNY: That's right, you are. *(To* GUY*)* Tell you what, you can be pal. How about that? *(To* JOEY*)* He's your baby brother now. You got to look out for him, take care of him.

*(*JOEY *kisses* GUY *on the head.)*

BENNY: That's my buddy.

(The flash goes off again, bright light. once again, GUY *grimaces.)*

BEBE: I think Guy wet himself.

LINDA: Oh for crying out loud!

BENNY: I got it. Don't worry about it.

LINDA: That's what Bebe's for.

BENNY: No. I'm his father now. That's what I'm for.

BEBE: You heard the man.

LINDA: Benny, I do believe you're a treasure.

*(*BENNY *takes* LINDA*'s hand, kisses it.)*

BENNY: You have made me so happy.

*(*LINDA *looks into* BENNY*'s eyes, wanting desperately to believe this.)*

LINDA: I have, haven't I?

BENNY: *(Looks around him)* And you'll all stay. Here. Safe with me.

LINDA: Well, Bebe's not really family.

JOEY: Bebe mine.

*(*BENNY *smiles.)*

BENNY: No one's leaving. Come on, a family picture. Everybody, get in.

(BENNY *aims the camera.* JOEY *sits on the couch, takes*
BEBE*'s hand who stands next to* LINDA, *crowding her.*)

LINDA: Got enough room there?

BEBE: Don't worry about me.

LINDA: Oh, I don't.

BEBE: I think Guy is crying.

BENNY: That's cause he's so happy.

LINDA: That must be it. Maybe I should be crying, too.
Oh Benny, love is the great redeemer, isn't it? Yes it is,
of course it is.

(BELLA *stands behind* JOEY, *behind a scrim wall.* BENNY,
sets the automatic timer on the camera.)

BENNY: This moment, this perfect little moment, me
with my family. It makes everything worthwhile.

LINDA: No regrets, Benny?

(BENNY *gently touches* LINDA*'s face.*)

BENNY: I wouldn't change a thing. The ends always
justify the means. Look at us, we're a family now. A
beautiful family.

(*This rag tag family softens, wanting desperatley to believe
that they are indeed a beautiful family.*)

LINDA: I can hardly believe it. I finally have my happy
ending and all appearances to the contrary, it's all I
ever wanted.

BEBE: Me too.

JOEY: Me too.

(BENNY *takes* GUY*'s head and nods it up and down in a "me
too" even as* GUY *quietly continues to cry.* JOEY *climbs into*
GUY*'s lap, and as he did for* BELLA, *begins to make cooing
sounds like a bird.*)

BENNY: Me too. Okay, everybody, big smile.

(*A blinding flash as the family smiles for the camera. the
lights bright on them. Lights out on them, and a single spot
appears on a sheet, and we see* BELLA'*s face, from behind it,
her broken smile as she looks down on her son. lights out on
her. The last sheet is lit with the words "one week ago". We
see* BENNY *sitting alone at a table, he takes out an envelope
of money and slides it across the table.*)

BENNY: Her name is Bella Cruz. I guess she would be
a co-worker of yours. I need you to kill her. I don't
want her to suffer, but I can't have her take my son
away from me. He's my world. And he needs me so
much. He's a great kid, too, a little problem with anger,
but hey, who doesn't have that? Remember, I don't
want her to suffer. Just kill her. That's all. Make her
disappear.

(BENNY *rises, takes the last sheet down, folds it, puts it
in the laundry basket. He sighs in contentment, takes the
laundry basket and enters the house, closing the door behind
him.*)

END OF PLAY

www.ingramcontent.com/pod-product-compliance
Lightning Source LLC
Chambersburg PA
CBHW052211090426
42741CB00010B/2495